David Álvarez
Burlington, V/2002

Sounds of a Cowhide Drum

Sounds of a Cowhide Drum

POEMS BY

OSWALD MBUYISENI MTSHALI

FOREWORD BY NADINE GORDIMER

THE THIRD PRESS

Joseph Okpaku Publishing Co., Inc.

444 Central Park West, New York, N.Y. 10025 U.S.A.

Library of Congress Catalogue Card Number: 73-183198

SBN: clothbound 89388-034-5
paperbound 89388-035-3

Designed by Bennie Arrington

First printing   Printed in the U.S.A.

For my late parents, especially my mother
who wanted me "to be something in life."

CONTENTS

FOREWORD

Many people write poetry, but there are few poets in any generation, in any country. There is a new poet in Africa, and his name is Oswald Mbuyiseni Mtshali.

Is he an African poet because he is black? Is he an English poet because he writes in English? Does he belong with Léopold Sédar Senghor of Senegal, Tchicaya U Tam'si of the Congo, Wole Soyinka and Christopher Okigbo of Nigeria, Jean-Joseph Rabearivelo of Madagascar, Mazisi Kunene, K.A. Nortje and Dennis Brutus of South Africa? Or do his songs of innocence and experience place him somewhere along with Blake, and his gifts of colloquial irony with the tradition of Auden, and his almost surgical imagery along with Sylvia Plath?

In an introduction to their collection of "Modern Poetry from Africa", Ulli Beier and Gerald Moore remark that it is dangerous to try and establish a literary orthodoxy. But they point out that the process of poetry is "essentially one of verbal magic: the poet-magus makes by naming. It (the process) undoubtedly lies at the root of all poetry, but it is probably closer to the surface of the poet's mind in Africa than elsewhere because of the recent arrival of literacy in the area, and because he inhabits a society where a vast body of traditional ritual, dance, song, poetry (spoken) and story is still alive." Mtshali has this verbal magic; for the reader he makes-by-naming areas of experience that, for fellow blacks, will provide a shock of recognition, and for whites, a revelation of a world they live in and never know. Only a fine poet could write so well; only an African could convey this experience. I don't think the synthesis has happened in quite this way before, in South Africa.

How does Oswald Mbuyiseni Mtshali see himself? If one looks carefully into the work of any poet, one will find his manifesto set out somewhere more succinctly than could be expressed in any analysis.

> Look upon me as a pullet crawling
> from an eggshell

        laid by a Zulu hen
        ready to fly in spirit
        to all lands on earth.

The colloquial tone, the ironic humour, the shackle of vivid,
concrete, regional-personal image, the liberation of imagination
that makes the creative writer freeman of the world—here in a
few lines is Mtshali's stylistic and philosophical statement.

Stylistically, it is not as simple as it looks. The simplicity—
balladic, lyrical, unerringly chosen acocrding to the demands
of the subject—is an end and not a beginning. That it has
been reached by labour and the priceless dissatisfactions of self-
criticism is evident in a few poems that I myself should have
left out of this book, but perhaps should be in it because, by con-
trast with the majority, they show how this poet has sloughed-
off what mars them: the grandiose invocation, "literary" image,
trite phrase. His best work is unadorned. It stands clear in the
surety of his verbal magic, at home in his own vocabulary.

Mtshali's relationship with his immediate world—his phil-
osophical approach, if you prefer—is married successfully with
his style. The most striking poems are often those where the
verbal magic—in this case the creation of mood or sense of
place—contains a sting that finally shrivels the verbal magic
away, leaving a question or statement burning in the mind. The
lovely evocative simplicity of "The Shepherd and His Flock",
which begins with

        The rays of the sun
        like a pair of scissors
        cutting the blanket
        of dawn from the sky

ends with a sudden insight into the mind of the boy greeting the
white farmer's children as they go to school: will he ever go to
school, too? In "Boy On a Swing", pure sensation is conveyed,
making-by-naming with heady brilliance, but out of the dis-
orientation-in-space of swinging, the "four cardinal points meet
in the boy's head" and the cardinal questions of the child's life
are flung out of the poem centrifugally:

Where did I come from?
When will I wear long trousers?
Why was my father jailed?

These questions, contained objectively in totally different categories, fuse together in the context of a black township child's life and thereby tell us everything we need to know about that life. When — not often — Mtshali turns to symbolism and metaphor, as in "Ride Upon the Death Chariot", where Caesar's empire is used as an equivalent for one nearer home, he slashes away with a single image the comfortable remove of history at which he has put us. The woman who comes to wipe the faces of the vagrants

> whose papers to be in Caesar's empire
> were not in order

is suddenly poignantly localised —

> She carried a dishcloth
> full of bread and tea.

Oswald Mbuyiseni Mtshali is the poet of the kraal peasant —

> thick-limbed labourers
> in vests baked
> brown with dust

— and the black miner —

> face
> daubed with gold-tinted ochre
> ... armpits mouldy with sweat of pushing a cocopan ...
> He shakes a plastic 'skal' in a noisy beerhall
> and gulps down the beer
> and strikes his chest,
> a victor over a day's work:
> "Hurray I'm the brawn —
> and you're the brain".

Mtshali has forgotten nothing of the black man's rural past, nor does he turn historical tragedy into costume-drama [compare the pith of his "Birth of Shaka" with the overblown rhetoric of Senghor's epic poem about Shaka.] But he is also—pre-eminently—the poet of the black Johannesburger, a Villon of Soweto, the voice of that

> itchy-footed man
> reeking from a beerhall
> shuffling to jail,
> swaying to hospital.

Township bully, roadganger, clerk, drunk, chauffeur, night-watchman

> (The jemmy boys
> have not paid him a visit
> but if they come
> he will die in honour,
> die fighting
> like a full-blooded Zulu—
> and the baas will say
> "Here's ten pounds.
> Jim was a good boy.")

—he sings of all these, and of their other, collective identity in the city as eternal suspect—for being poor, for being black, for rousing guilt:

> I trudge the city pavements
> side by side with "madam"
> who shifts her handbag
> from my side to the other . . .

This is a city poet's tongue, quick as a chamelon's and rasping as a tiger's. The white man's conscience may be "locked safely with bonds and securities in a Chubb safe sarcophagus" but perhaps the white man's skin may not be quite impervious to irony.

The world you will enter through these poems is a black man's world made by white men. It finds its epitome in the ghastly vision of township dogs fighting over the corpse of an abandoned baby — surely one of the most shocking poems ever written, and yet a triumph, since it could have been achieved only by forging from bitterness a steely compassion, by plunging into horror deep enough to bring forth tenderness. If, in this world, the poet Mtshali belongs automatically to an elite, it is the dead-end elite into which black artists and intellectuals are thrust by any colour-bar society. The daily circumstances of his life remain those of the majority population of South Africa. The image of bread recurs again and again in his work: even snow suggests the labour for bread — "Trees sagged and grunted under the back-breaking flour bags of snow" and the fact that man cannot live by bread alone is seen as a need for the "rare bread, solitude" which he seeks to

> feed my hunger to read
> to dream, and to write.

This is the imagery of survival. Oswald Mtshali, ironist, knows all that threatens man, abroad as well as at home: the Berlin walls of distrust, and the "moats of fright around his heart". He knows, finally, that even man's apparent virtues threaten him, in some times and places. In "An Old Man in Church", where a black labourer

> drinks the Lord's blood from a golden chalice
> with cracked lips thirsty for peace . . .
> his ears enraptured by rustling silk vestments of the priest,

the last line is not Mtshali's at all, but in this context one of the most ironic ever written:

> Blessed are the meek for they shall inherit the earth.

NADINE GORDIMER
JOHANNESBURG, 1971

Sounds of a Cowhide Drum

THE SHEPHERD AND HIS FLOCK

The rays of the sun
are like a pair of scissors
cutting the blanket
of dawn from the sky.

The young shepherd
drives the master's sheep
from the paddock
into the veld.

His bare feet kick the grass
and spill the dew
like diamonds
on a cutter's table.
A lamb strays away
enchanted by the marvels
of a summer morning;
the ram
rebukes the ewe,
"Woman! Woman!
Watch over the child!"

The sun wings up
on flaming petals
of a sunflower.

He perches on an antheap
to play the reed flute,
and to salute
the farmer's children
going to school,
and dreamily asks,
"O! Wise Sun above,
will you ever guide
me into school?"

I WILL TELL IT TO MY WITCHDOCTOR

I will tell it all
to the witchdoctor,
as I sit on a mat
of woven grass and beads;
and dry monkey bones
shrink my head
and rattle the eardrums.

I will listen to his voice
chanting incantations
like a priest giving a blessing
to a soul seeking solace.

I will ask him
to boil a pot of herbs,
and brew a love potion
as strong as a mule's milk.

I will give it
to the world
whose eyes are myopic with misery;
and this world will wink a smile,
and dandle me like a devoted mother,
and smother me with affection
I have never known before.

BOY ON A SWING

Slowly he moves
to and fro, to and fro,
then faster and faster
he swishes up and down.

His blue shirt
billows in the breeze
like a tattered kite.

The world whirls by:
east becomes west,
north turns to south;
the four cardinal points
meet in his head.

      Mother!
Where did I come from?
When will I wear long trousers?
Why was my father jailed?

PORTRAIT OF A LOAF OF BREAD

Look back to the rolling fields
waving gold-topped wheat stalks
mowed by the reaper's scythe,
bundled into sheaves
carted to the mill
and ground into flour.
      Kneaded into mountains of dough
      to be churned by rollers
      and spat into pans as red hot
      as Satan's cauldron.

Brought to the café,
warmly wrapped in cellophane,
by "Eat Fresh Bread" bakery van;
for the waiting cook
to slice and toast
to butter and to marmalade
for the food-bedecked breakfast table.

While the labourer
with fingers caked with
wet cement of a builder's scaffold
mauls a hunk and a cold drink
and licks his lips and laughs
"Man can live on bread alone."

THE WASHERWOMAN'S PRAYER
(To My Mother-in-Law)

Look at her hands
raw, knobbly and calloused.
Look at her face
Like a bean skin soaked in brine.

For countless years she has toiled
to wash her master's clothes
Soiled by a lord's luxuries.

In frost-freckled mornings,
In sun-scorched afternoons,
She has drudged murmurless.

One day she fell and fainted
With weariness.
Her mouth a foaming spout
Gushing a gibberish.

"Good Lord! Dear Lord!" she shouted
"Why am I so tormented?
How long have I lamented?
Tell me Lord, tell me O Lord."

"My child! Dear child", she heard,
"Suffer for those who live in gilded sin,
Toil for those who swim in a bowl of pink gin."

"Thank you Lord! Thank you Lord.
Never again will I ask
Why must I carry this task."

A SNOWFALL ON MOUNT FRERE

Puffed up peaks
were a Kit-Kat loaf
covered with unsweet
icing sugar;
ready for aproned sunshine
to slice it.

Trees sagged
and grunted
under the back-breaking
flour bags of snow.
Breathless
they cursed and waited
for sunrays
to lift their burden.

The weak-eyed sun
peered through the curtained sky
on to the papery whiteness.
She blinked;
then went back
to fetch her reading glasses.

Mud huts sprouted
on the vastness;
a rash of blackheads;
on the heavily-powdered
face of a woman.

Red wide-horned cows
plonked belly-deep in quilt
like famished bed bugs
some snorted steamy defiance
to the scowling sky.

Birds huddled helplessly
against the whiplashing wind;
and raised their frozen feeble voices
in protest to the skulking sun.

No tribesmen
ventured out.
They were marooned
in their hearthless huts
by the vast white sea.
They cringed like drowning gorillas
chained in cold steel cages.

MEN IN CHAINS

The train stopped
at a country station,

Through sleep-curtained eyes
I peered through the frosty window,
and saw six men:
men shorn
of all human honour
like sheep after shearing,
bleating at the blistering wind,
"Go away! Cold wind! Go away!
Can't you see we are naked?"

They hobbled into the train
on bare feet,
wrists handcuffed,
ankles manacled
with steel rings like cattle at the abbatoirs
shying away from the trapdoor.

One man with a head
shaven clean as a potato
whispered to the rising sun,
a red eye wiped by a tattered
handkerchief of clouds,
"Oh! Dear Sun!
Won't you warm my heart
with hope?"
The train went on its way to nowhere.

INSIDE MY ZULU HUT

It is a hive
without any bees
to build the walls
with golden bricks of honey.
A cave cluttered
with a millstone,
calabashes of sour milk
claypots of foaming beer
sleeping grass mats
wooden head rests
tanned goat skins
tied with riempies
to wattle rafters
blackened by the smoke
of kneaded cow dung
burning under
the three-legged pot
on the earthen floor
to cook my porridge.

calabash gourd, dried and holowed out, traditionally used for storing
liquids.

REAPERS IN A MIELIEFIELD

Faces furrowed and wet with sweat,
Bags tied to their wasp waists,
women reapers bend *mielie* stalks,
break cobs in rustling sheaths,
toss them in the bags
and move through row upon row of maize.

Behind them, like a desert tanker,
a dust-raising tractor
pulls a trailer,
driven by a pipe-puffing man
flashing tobacco-stained teeth
as yellow as the harvested grain.

He stops to pick up bags
loaded by thick-limbed labourers
in vests baked
brown with dust.

The sun lashes
the workers with
a red-hot rod;
they stop for a while
to wipe a brine-bathed brow
and drink from battered cans
bubbling with malty *maheu*

Thirst is slaked in seconds,
Men jerk bags like feather cushions
and women become prancing wild mares;
soon the day's work will be done
and the reapers will rest in their kraals.

mielie   maize (Afrikaans).
maheu   mielie meal gruel, slightly fermented and drunk cold (Zulu).
kraal   African village (Afrikaans).

A NEWLY-BORN CALF

A newly-born calf
is like oven-baked bread
steaming under a cellophane cover.
The cow cuts
the shiny coat
as a child would
lick a toffee
with a tongue as pink as
the sole of a foot.
The calf sways on legs
filled with jelly and custard
instead of bone and marrow;
and it totters
to suck the teats
of its mother's udder.

THE BIRTH OF SHAKA

His baby cry
was of a cub
tearing the neck
of the lioness
because he was fatherless.

The gods
boiled his blood
in a clay pot of passion
to course in his veins.

His heart was shaped into an ox shield
to foil every foe.

Ancestors forged
his muscles into
thongs as tough
as wattle bark
and nerves
as sharp as
syringa thorns.

His eyes were lanterns
that shone from the dark valleys of Zululand
to see white swallows
coming across the sea.
His cry to two assassin brothers:

"Lo! you can kill me
but you'll never rule this land!"

A ROADGANG'S CRY

Pneumatic drills
roar like guns in a battle field
as they tear the street.

Puffing machines swallow the red soil
and spit it out like a tuberculotic's sputum.

Business-bent brokers hurry past;
Women shoppers shamble tiredly, shooing their children;
Stragglers stop to stare
as the ruddy-faced foreman watches men
lifting a sewerage pipe into a trench.

It starts
as a murmur
from one mouth to another
in a rhythm of ribaldry
that rises to a crescendo
*"Abelungu ngo'dam
Basibiza ngo Jim*

Whites are damned
they call us Jim."

THE RAIN IN THE VELD

He dripped like an unpreened cat
tossed by a prankster's hand
into a tubful of icy water
chilling the bones and setting
the marrow into an unsalted broth;
licked the laughing lips
jellied by a cold mucus
flowing from an unwiped nose.
To be a young capering cowherd
with an empty billycan buckled to the belt
and driving a homeward-bound herd
of robust cows with hides steambathing
blood-gorged ticks, and frisking calves with
nostrils spurting steam jets, O! so cavorting carefree.

WALLS

Man is
a great wall builder
the Berlin Wall
the Wailing Wall of Jerusalem
but the wall
most impregnable
has a moat
flowing with fright
around his heart.

A wall
without windows
for the spirit
to breeze through

A wall
without a door
for love to walk in.

PIGEONS IN THE OPPENHEIMER PARK

I wonder why these pigeons in the Oppenheimer Park
are never arrested and prosecuted for trespassing
on private property and charged with public indecency.

Every day I see these insolent birds perched
on "Whites Only" benches, defying all authority.
Don't they know of the Separate Amenities Act?
A white policeman in full uniform, complete
with a holstered .38 special, passes by
without even raising a reprimanding finger
at offenders who are flouting the law.
They not only sit on the hallowed benches,
they also mess them up with birdshit.

Oh! Holy Ideology! look at those two at the crest
of the jumping impala, they are making love in full
view of madams, hobos, giggling office girls.
What is the world coming to?
Where's the sacred Immorality Act? *Sies!*

Sies Afrikaans exclamation of disgust (pronounced to rhyme with "hiss").

A VOICE FROM THE DEAD

I heard it
in my sleep
calling me softly.

It was
my mother
speaking from her grave.

My son!
there is no heaven
above the clouds.

WHAT!

Yes, Heaven is in your heart.
God is no picture
With a snow-white beard.

WHAT!

Yes, God is
that crippled beggar
sprawling at the street corner.

There is no hell burning
with sulphur and brimstone.

WHAT!

Yes, Hell is
the hate flickering
in your eye.

A BRAZIER IN THE STREET

Around the smoke-billowing brazier
huddled four urchins, smoking
cigarette stubs and swopping stories
like seamen telling tales over a bottle of rum.
> The wintry air nipped their navels
> as a calf would suck the nipple.
> Smoke, blowing into bleary eyes,
> and waving flames fashioned
> their bodies into crouching silhouettes.
One yawned —
and rubbed his sleep-laden eyes
and mumbled as if in a dream
"I once ate a loaf of bread with nothing . . . ."

Then a buxom woman, blanketed
against the blistering chill,
came out of the house
and carried the red-hot brazier inside
to cook her supper.

And quicker than a rabid dog
leaps to swallow its tail,
the starless night gaped
and gulped down the foursome.

AN OLD MAN IN CHURCH

I know an old man
who during the week is a machine working at full throttle:
productivity would stall,
spoil the master's high profit estimate,
if on Sunday he did not go to church
to recharge his spiritual batteries.

He never says his prayer in a velvet-cushioned pew —
it would only be a whisper on God's ear.
He falls on raw knees
that smudge the bare floor with his piety.
He hits God's heart with screams as hard as stones
flung from the slingshot of his soul.
He takes the gilded communion plate with gnarled hands,
he lowers his eyes into the deep pond of serenity,
his brow rippling with devotion,
his ears enraptured by rustling silk vestments of the priest.
He drinks the Lord's blood from a golden chalice
with cracked lips thirsty for peace.

The acolyte comes around with a brass-coated

                                         collection plate

the old man sneaks in a cent piece
that raises a scowl on the collector's face
whose puckered nose sneezes at such poor generosity
instead of inhaling the aromatic incense smoke.
Then the preacher stands up in the pulpit
his voice fiery with holy fervour:
"Blessed are the meek for they shall inherit the earth."

THE DAY WE BURIED OUR BULLY

Through years and years
of harrassment
we tolerated his hideous deeds:
    girls abducted,
    women molested,
    boys assaulted,
    and men robbed.

Our fear made him our master.

One day
old warrior Death
whipped out his .38 special
from its holster
and felled our tormentor with a single shot.

We turned his corpse
into a piece of meat
tucked in between
the sandwich of soil
black like burnt toast
ready for ants and worms
to eat for breakfast
and excrete as manure.

We laid wreaths
of withered flowers
to fill his grave
with an odour of decay
wafted by the wind,

As mourners smiled
through tears of relief,
"Lord! take care of his soul—
though he was but a bully."

A LOST COIN

It lies shimmering on the pavement
like a drop of molten lead.

Pedestrians
blind like bats in the sunshine
flit past.

An urchin
rummaging for cigarette stubs
scoops it up,
and rushes to a Greek cafe —
bread for life?
sweet for joy? —
a chocolate slab
of Happiness
to be swallowed in a gulp
into an empty tummy,
and come out as sweet nothingness
in an alley toilet.

SUNSET

The sun spun like
a tossed coin.
It whirled on the azure sky,
it clattered into the horizon,
it clicked in the slot,
and neon-lights popped
and blinked "Time expired",
as on a parking meter.

THIS KID IS NO GOAT

Where have
All the angry young men gone?
Gone to the Island of Lament for Sharpeville.
Gone overseas on scholarship,
Gone up North to milk and honeyed uhuru.
Gone to the dogs with the drink of despair.

Yesterday I met one in a bookstore:
he was foraging for food for thought
from James Baldwin, Le Roi Jones
Albert Camus, Jean-Paul Sartre.

He wore faded jeans and heavy sweater,
he saluted me with a
        "Hi! brother!"
He was educated in a country mission school
where he came out clutching a rosary
as an amulet against
        Slegs vir Blankes — For Whites Only."

He enrolled at Life University
whose lecture rooms were shebeens,
hospital wards and prison cells.

He graduated *cum laude*
with a thesis in philosophy:
"I can't be black and straight
in this crooked white world!"
If I tell the truth
I'm detestable.
If I tell lies
I'm abominable.
If I tell nothing
I'm unpredictable.
If I smile to please
I'm nothing but an obsequious sambo.

I have adopted jazz as my religion
with Duke Ellington, Count Basie,
Louis Armstrong as my High Priests.
No more do I go to church
where the priest has left me in the lurch.
His sermon is a withered leaf
falling from a decaying pulpit-tree
to be swept away
by violent gusts of doubt and scepticism.

"My wife and kids can worship there:
they want to go to heaven when they die.
I don't want to go to heaven when I'm dead.
I want my heaven now,
here on earth in Houghton and Parktown;
a mansion
two cars or more
and smiling servants.
Isn't that heaven?"

RIDING ON THE RAINBOW*

Boom! Boom! Boom!
the bass rumbles, trumpet screams,
cymbals hiss, sax moans, the piano clanks.

And off I go
streaking across the sky like David's slingshot
hitting "The Giants"
into the rainbow's face.

Up and up
on a wild horse of jazz
we galloped on a network
of blue notes
delivering the message:
Men, Brothers, Giants!

* With the Jazz Giants at the first public reading, May 22, 1968—ed.

HIGH AND LOW

Glorious is this world,
the world that sustains man
like a maggot in a carcass.

Mighty is the sea
de-salted by the carapace in the eye of a fish.

Hallowed is the star,
effulgent in the firmament,
a pearl in the stomach of a mussel sky.

Majestic soars the eagle, golden winged above the low life.

Black is the hole of the poet,
a mole burrowing from no entrance to no exit.

ALWAYS A SUSPECT

I get up in the morning
and dress up like a gentleman—
A white shirt a tie and a suit.

I walk into the street
to be met by a man
who tells me to "produce."

I show him
the document of my existence
to be scrutinized and given the nod.

Then I enter the foyer of a building
to have my way barred by a commissionaire
"What do you want?"

I trudge the city pavements
side by side with "madam"
who shifts her handbag
from my side to the other,
and looks at me with eyes that say
"Ha! Ha! I know who you are;
beneath those fine clothes
ticks the heart of a thief."

KEEP OFF THE GRASS

The grass is a green mat
trimmed with gladioli
red like flames in a furnace.
The park bench, hallowed,
holds the loiterer listening
to the chant of the fountain
showering holy water on a congregation
of pigeons.

Keep off the grass,
Dogs not under leash forbidden.

Then madam walks her Pekinese,
bathed and powdered and perfumed.
He sniffs at the face of the "Keep Off" sign
with a nose as cold as frozen fish
and salutes it with a hind paw
leaving it weeping in anger and shame.

THE CHAUFFEUR SHUFFLE

He sits grim-faced
like a carving of blackwood
in a peaked cap,
clutching the wheel
with white gloved hands,
his eyes glued to the road ahead.

Behind him snarls
his tiger passenger
glaring through the window,
peering at the wristwatch
as the city-bound traffic
files into a bumper-to-bumper queue.

Though the limousine
limps like a man
tormented by corns,
the driver remains
as unruffled as a duck
in a pond,
and wades his way into town.

On the back seat
Vesuvius hisses
a last sigh of smouldering —
"John! stop here,
I'll get off" —
and darts out,
briefcase in hand,
to keep the first
appointment of the day.

AT THE SEASHORE

The money-laden landlubber
sneezes out the gold dust
rising like a cloud
from the mine dump.

He scurries
to the coast
like a rabbit from hounds;
books at the beachfront hotel,
sits in the sun
rolls on the sandy carpet
woven with beads of seashells;
and turns into a statue
of bronzed biceps.

The sea breeze
wafts a spray
of air into lungs
heavy with cobwebs
of cigar smoke.

The ear listens
to the waves
singing a lullaby:
"The sea O! the sea,
to soothe the soul
of the surfeited pleasure-seeker."

His eye jumps into life
to devour the body
of a bikini girl
cavorting like a mare
looking for a stallion.

The day ends
at the patio of the hotel
where a waiter
grins through thick lips,
bringing ice-cold beer
for the master and missus.

A DRUNK IN THE STREET

When you see him sprawled in the gutter,
his fly open, his mouth dripping with vomit,
his eyes bloodshot with booze,
spit into his face and pass on.

Your sputum is a golden gossamer
hanging on his eyelashes, festooned
with visions of a fat spider
sitting in a Persian carpeted room
counting piles and piles of money.

The spider tosses a coin to the fallen man.
He picks it up and crawls on his knees
red and raw with hot urine.

He tells beads
on his broken toes as a holy rosary.

"O! money-god
floating in your celestial cobweb
blessed be thy tossed coins
for opening a beerhall barrel
to quench my sizzling thirst. Amen."

THE MOULTING COUNTRY BIRD

I wish
I was not a bird
red and tender of body
with the mark of the tribe
branded on me as a fledgling
hatched in the Zulu grass hut.

Pierced in the lobe of the ear
by the burning spike of the elderman;
he drew my blood like a butcher bird
that impales the grasshopper on the thorn.

As a full fledged starling
hopping in the city street,
scratching the building corridor,
I want to moult
from the dung-smeared down
tattered like a fieldworker's shirt,
tighter than the skin of a snake
that sleeps as the plough turns the sod.

Boots caked with mud,
wooden stoppers flapping from earlobes
and a beaded little gourd dangling on a hirsute chest,
all to stoke the incinerator.

I want to be adorned
by a silken suit so scintillating in sheen,
it pales even the peacock's plumage,
and catches the enchanted eye
of a harlot hiding in an alley:
"Come! my moulten bird,
I will not charge you a price!"

THE SONG OF SUNRISE

The sword of daybreak
snips the shroud
of the night from the sky,
and the morning
peeps through the blankets
like a baby rising
from its cot
to listen to the
peal of the bell.

Arise! Arise!
All Workers!
To work! To work!
You must go!

Buses rumble,
Trains rattle,
Taxis hoot.

I shuffle in the queue
with feet that patter
on the station platform,
and stumble into the coach
that squeezes me like a lemon
of all the juice of my life.

PORTRAIT OF AN OLD PAIR OF SHOES

Tanned as a hide of a hefty heifer,
carved by the craftsman's scalpel,
and shined to a shimmering blackness
as of liquid tar piping hot.

To go through life
carrying an itchy-footed man
reeking from a beerhall
shuffling to jail
swaying to hospital.

Scuffed to a decrepit state
of soles stabbed by daggers of wanderlust,
then abandoned on a city pavement,
waiting to be carted by the refuse remover's truck
for a pauper's funeral in a dumping ground.

THE MINER

At the strike of the noon bell
he pops out of the shaft
like a pea shot from the muzzle of a bazooka.

He plods on iron-spiked boots
to stretch limbs on a coir-Mattress bed in the compound,

With gnarled hands
Daubed with gold-tinted ochre
to wash a face
and armpits mouldy with sweat of pushing a cocopan
down the rails into the ore-crushing mill.

He shakes a plastic *skal* in a noisy beerhall
and gulps down the beer
and strikes his chest,
a victor over a day's work:
"Hurray I'm the brawn —
And you're the brain".

cocopan small vehicles on rails, used in mines for transporting ore and
  debris.
coir mattress springless mattress stuffed with coconut fiber.
skal large drinking vessel used for beer (township argot).

TWO CHIMNEY SWEEPERS

I saw
two chimney sweeps
scraping the soot
inside a stack.

They came out
and wiped
their faces
and one said to the other
"I'm white and
I'll always stay so.
You're black
You'll remain so!"

THE FACE OF HUNGER

I counted ribs on his concertina chest
bones protruding as if chiselled
by a sculptor's hand of famine.

He looked with glazed pupils
seeing only a bun on some sky-high shelf.

The skin was pale and taut
like a glove on a doctor's hand.

His tongue darted in and out
like a chameleon's
snatching a confetti of flies.

O! child,
your stomach is a den of lions
roaring day and night.

IF YOU SHOULD KNOW ME

Once concealed
like the Devil
in the body
of a serpent —
as an apple of sin
in the hand
of a temptress —
I am the biter.

For all
I bare my heart
to see the flint
to be ignited
into a flame
shaped like three tongues
that tell me —
look, listen and learn
what surrounds me.

O! come search
my soul for non-existent virtues
outnumbered by vices
as numerous as greenflies
devouring all my righteousness.

Look upon me as a pullet crawling
from an eggshell
laid by a Zulu hen,
ready to fly in spirit
to all lands on earth.

INTAKE NIGHT — BARAGWANATH HOSPITAL

The ward was like a battlefield —
victims of war
waged in the dark alley
flocked in cars, taxis, ambulances, vans and trucks.

They bore
knife wounds
axe wounds
bullet wounds
burns and lacerations.

A stench
of fresh blood
warm urine
excreta,
mingled with iodine and methylated spirits.

Groans
sighs
moans — Help me doctor help!
Curse — C'mon bloody nurse!

Doctors darting
from place to place
with harried nurses at their side.
"So! it's Friday night!
Everybody's enjoying
in Soweto."

ON DROWNING SORROW
(*Reflections of a Man*)

Where do I drown my sorrows
if not in the drum
of wine, whiskey and beer?
On it I skim like a waterfly
sending ripples of sympathy
around the world for goodwill.

With what do I blunt my feelings
if not with the weed wrapped in the green seed
crackling in the brown paper greased with saliva?

How do I satisfy
my instintcs as hot as cinders,
if not with tender flesh of a female
flushed with blood as I squeeze her breasts
and caress her thighs!

All sorrows
are banished now —
but woe when they return
to capture my soul!

NIGHTFALL IN SOWETO

Nightfall comes like
a dreaded disease
seeping through the pores
of a healthy body
and ravaging it beyond repair.

A murderer's hand,
lurking in the shadows,
clasping the dagger
strikes down the helpless victim.
I am the victim.

I am slaughtered
every night in the streets.
I am cornered by the fear
gnawing at my timid heart;
in my helplessness I languish.

Man has ceased to be man
Man has become beast
Man has become prey.
I am the prey.

I am the quarry to be run down
by the marauding beast
let loose by cruel nightfall
from his cage of death.

Where is my refuge?
Where am I safe?
Not in my matchbox house
where I barricade myself against nightfall.

Soweto the huge conglomeration of dormitory "suburbs" reserved for
  Africans "appended" to Johannesburg: its population is variously given
  as between 500,000 and 1,000,000.

I tremble at his crunching footsteps,
I quake at his deafening knock at the door.
"Open up!" he barks like a rabid dog
thirsty for my blood.

Nightfall! Nightfall!
You are my mortal enemy.
But why were you ever created?
Why can't it be daytime?
Daytime forever more?

AT HEAVEN'S DOOR

Something
is not right
there upstairs,
maybe the wrong
is down here.

I have
been knocking
at the Door
since I learned
how to pray.

There
is only silence.
Where are the servants —
I mean the angels?

I don't see them
peering through curtains
to see who is calling.

When
the Master at last
says
      "Come in,"

Will they
let me in
through the front
or at the back entrance?

THE COFFIN

There it stand glistering
like a well-polished coach
of mahogany, silver handled,
waiting to carry any paying
passenger on a long, long journey
to a destination of resurrection or perdition.
The fare is the traveller's life,
to be paid before the trip starts.

Soon it comes to a newly-completed house
with an up "Vacant" notice:
"Ready for immediate occupation
by any permanent tenant,
all welcome, the young and old
the rich and poor, the powerful and weak."

THE WATCHMAN'S BLUES

High up
in the loft of a skyscraper
above the penthouse of the potentate,
he huddles
in his nest by day: by night
he is an owl that descends,
knobkierie in hand
to catch the rats that come
to nibble the treasure-strewn street windows.

He sits near a brazier,
his head bobbing like a fish cork
in the serene waters of sleep.

The jemmy boys
have not paid him a visit,
but if they come
he will die in honour,
die fighting
like a full-blooded Zulu—
and the *baas* will say:
"Here's ten pounds.
Jim was a good boy."

To rise and keep awake
and twirl the kierie
and shoo the wandering waif
and chase the hobo with *"Voetsak"*.

knobkierie knobbed stick or club (Afrikaans)
jemmy boys burglars armed with crow-bars
Voetsak "Be off", with an implication of contempt (Afrikaans)

To wait for the rays of the sun
to spear the fleeing night,
while he pines
for the three wives and a dozen children
sleeping alone in the kraal
far away in the majestic mountains
of Mahlabathim—
"Where I'm a man
amongst men,
not John or Jim
but Makhubalo Magudulela."

THE DETRIBALISED

He was born in Sophiatown,
Or Alexandra, I am not sure,
but certainly not in Soweto.

He skipped school
during playtime
to hock sweets
peanuts, shoelaces,
pilfered in town,
caddied at the golfcourse.

He can write —
only his name;
He can read —
The World:
"Our one and only paper",
The Golden City Post —
murder, rape and robbery.

He has served time
at the "Fort".
Prison is no shame,
just as unavoidable
and unpleasant
as going to a dentist.

He's a "clever"
not a "moegie";
he never says baas
to no bloody white man.

He wears
the latest Levison's suits
"Made in America";
from Cuthbert's
a pair of Florscheim shoes

the Fort   the main prison in Johannesburg
moegie   bumpkin (township argot)

"America's finest shoes"
He pays cash
that's why
he's called Mister.

He goes for quality, man,
not quantity, never—
the price is no obstacle.

His furniture is
from Ellis, Bradlow's, exclusive.

Nothing from the O.K. Bazaars
except groceries
and Christmas toys
for their kids.
"Very cheap!" says his wife.

Yes, his wife—
also born in the city, Orlando!
she's pretty,
dresses very well:
costumes from Vanité or Millews.

She's very sophisticated,
uses Artra, Hi-Lite
skin lightening cream,
hair straightened,
wears lipstick
a wig, nail polish:
she can dance
the latest "Monkey".

He married her
after he had fathered
two kids
to prove her fertility.
There's the occasional
domestic quarrel:
he punches her
a "blue eye"
to show her
he's the boss.

He takes another cherie
to the movies
at Lyric or Majestic.
They dine at the Kapitan
and sleep at the Planet.

Maybe they go
to a night session
in a posh shebeen:
jazz, booze
knives and guns.

The wife sees
a *nyanga*
to bring her man back home.

He runs a car —
'60 Impala Chev.
Automatic, sleek.

He knows
he must carry a pass.
He don't care for politics
He don't go to church
He knows Sobukwe
he knows Mandela
They're in Robben Island.
"So what? That's not my business!"

Nyanga   (witch) doctor (Zulu)
Sobukwe   Robert Sobukwe, imprisoned leader of the banned Pan-African Congress
Mandela   Nelson Mandela, also imprisoned, a leader of the also banned African National Congress
Robben Island   the island prison off the coast of Cape Town where African political prisoners serving long terms are held.

GOING TO WORK

I go to work
for five days a week
with a thousand black bodies
encased in eleven coaches
that hurtle through stations
into the red ribbon of dawn
crowning the city skyscrapers.

A commuter mumbles
like a dreamer muffled
by a brandy nightcap
'Brothers, who doesn't know me . . .?
I'm a cog in Mr. Jobstein's wheel,
And Mr. Jobstein is a big wheel
Rolling under Mr. de Wiel's oxwaggon.'

MY METAMORPHOSIS

Once,
I was a sapling of a boy
luxuriating in the garden of adventure
watered by the inebriating shebeen tap;
my feet were youthful roots
which ran wild in search of self-atisfaction
and produced a branchful of knowledge.

Then,
I landed in a prison cell
where introspection gnawed at my heart
like a rat on a chunk of cheese.
For six months I lived with them —
murderers, rapists and robbers —
on our eyes hung a shroud of misery,
our cheeks were pages on which was written the law
of defiance to all forms of authority;
were were comrades in crime and intrigue.

Now,
perpetually at prayer while constantly cursing,
I am a mouse of sublimation,
introvert, waiting for night's cover
when I can pillage the cupboard
of my rare bread, solitude
and feed my hunger to read,
to dream, and to write.

WHITE CITY JABAVU*

I don't see
anything white
in this White City —
just the blackness
of widows' garments
of mourning.

Maybe the only
whiteness is
of a waif's teeth that chatter
in the hungry month.

Or the
white eye-ball
of a plundered corpse,
lying in the gutter.

Around me
is the gloomy
street corner
where dark figures
dart to deal
a deadly blow
on passersby.

I hear
women scream
in sorrow and despair
drying the gay rivers
of carousers.

I *stop*
to ponder
but what is white
in White City Jabavu?

*One of the townships of Soweto.

A BALLAD OF ELOFF STREET

Down there a road gang pecks
with picks and shovels
to the beat of a work song.

Tears of tar and dust
mix with rivers of sweat
on a broken brow.

The words of the song rise
in a crescendo higher and higher
to the dizzy height of an office window
where airconditioned executives sip
chilled beer or whisky on the rocks
and make love to their blushing secretaries

on luxury couches.

The setting sun comes peeping through curtained windows;
it scratches with talons of an eagle
for consciences
locked safely with bonds and securities
in a Chubb safe sarcophagus.

A street cleaner picks papers with a palsied hand,
shovels them into his satchel
as if to cook for supper on a stove box marked
"Keep your city clean,
Hou u stad skoon."

Clean!
Clean of what?
When a blind beggar sits at a street corner
and strums his battered guitar
and sings
"Though I'm blind
My soul can see."

Here where a pickpocket snatches
a wallet, a purse, and flees into an alley.

Where gawking yokels,
their shoes caked with cowdung,
come flying like moths to the bright city lights,
only to have their wings clipped
by the smooth-tongued confidence tricksters.

Where passes a pair of nut brown babies,
two flesh pedlars on a nocturnal stroll:
they jingle ample breasts and buttocks —
        "Wares up for sale."

THE MASTER OF THE HOUSE

Master, I am a stranger to you,
but will you hear my confession?

I am a faceless man
who lives in the backyard
of your house.

I share your table
so heavily heaped with
bread, meat and fruit
it huffs like a horse
drawing a coal cart.

As the rich man's to Lazarus,
the crumbs are swept to my lap
by my Lizzie:
"Sweetie! eat and be satisfied now,
To-morrow we shall be gone."

So nightly I run the gauntlet,
wrestle with your mastiff, Caesar,
for the bone pregnant with meat
and wash it down with Pussy's milk.

I am the nocturnal animal
that steals through the fenced lair
to meet my mate,
and flees at the break of dawn
before the hunter and the hounds
run me to ground.

JUST A PASSERBY

I saw them clobber him with kieries,
I heard him scream with pain
like a victim of slaughter;
I smelt fresh blood gush
from his nostrils,
and flow on the street.

I walked into the church,
and knelt in the pew,
'Lord! I love you,
I also love my neighbour. Amen.'

I came out
my heart as light as an angel's kiss
on the cheek of a saintly soul.

Back home I strutted
past a crowd of onlookers.
Then she came in —
my woman neighbour:
'Have you heard? They've killed your brother.'
'Oh! No! I heard nothing. I've been to church.'

HANDCUFFS

Handcuffs
have steel fangs
whose bite is more painful
than a whole battalion
of fleas.

Though the itch in my heart
grows deeper and deeper
I cannot scratch.

How can I?
my wrists
are manacled.
My mind
is caged.
My soul
is shackled.

I can only grimace at the ethereal cloud,
a banner billowing in the sky, emblazoned,
"Have hope, brother,
despair is for the defeated."

AT A SNAIL'S PACE, PLEASE

At the tip
of a chameleon's tongue
there is a pot of boiling glue
to cook flies for breakfast
before he sets off
on a slow tightwire walk
like a trapeze artist.

Under the belly of every snail
lies a tank full of low-octane petrol
to propel the miniscule engine
to a destination of a juicy cabbage leaf.

It is overtaken
by American mechanical monsters,
drunk with gallons of gasoline,
that leave highways strewn
with gory confetti of corpses.

The loud Bang!
brings brawny farmers
running from homesteads to render help.

From beehive huts tumble black bumpkins
to gawk at twisted wrecks coated with fresh blood
amid cries of "Help!'

Ambulances sound shrill sirens,
tearing the silky shawl of the night's silence.
O! speed fiend
whose knell has sounded,
look at the snail
slumbering
in his shell.
See the chameleon
cosy under her quilted coat.

MY SHADOW, COURAGE

My shadow is a fox-terrier named Courage;
it follows me wherever I go,
it snarls and snaps at all gremlins
that lie in my path waiting to ambush me;
it stops to sniff, sneeze and piss on a telegraph pole,
and leave a message for every potential follower,
"I passed here; follow if you dare".

Alas! that night I heard "The knock"—
it was at the door of my heart,
the knock that deflates your balls,
the knock that makes your hair roots
run tip-toed in circles on your head.

Oh! Courage! you deserted me,
you tucked your tail under the legs
and crept into a ragged bed of fleas
leaving my nakedness exposed.
I shivered for the snake suit
shed in the grass.
Fingers digging at the sockets,
my eyes flew with fear
and teardrops parachuted out.

A nose poked the navel with a deep stick
and out fled a pair of laughing lice
giggling like benzine drunk urchins
evicted from my bountiful pantry of poems.

I looked at my watch,
it was long past midnight.
My teeth itched to sew a thread
on a piece of bread-and-soup.
My hand groped for the doorknob of daybreak
and the morning mist smacked my face awake.
I looked at myself.
There I was. Shadowless there I was.
Empty like a hulk
waiting for a demolition squad.

O! Courage have you forsaken me forever?

AN ABANDONED BUNDLE

The morning mist
and chimney smoke
of White City Jabavu
flowed thick yellow
as pus oozing
from a gigantic sore.

It smothered our little houses
like fish caught in a net.

Scavenging dogs
draped in red bandanas of blood
fought fiercely
for a squirming bundle.

I threw a brick;
they bared fangs
flicked velvet tongues of scarlet
and scurried away,
leaving a mutilated corpse —
an infant dumped on a rubbish heap —
"Oh! Baby in the Manger
sleep well
on human dung."

Its mother
had melted into the rays of the rising sun,
her face glittering with innocence
her heart as pure as untrampled dew.

DEATH — THE TART
(*Written after the murder of Advocate Dan Kutumela*)

Dying
has become
the mistress
with whom we
brazenly carry on
an illicit love affair
that ends only
in the grave.

We rise
and kiss her
"Good morning my love"
and walk with her
hand in hand
into trains infested
with tsotsis.

We flirt
as we eat fish and chips
on a city pavement
whilst human blood
and torrents of tears flow.

Into this raging river
a passing hobo
hurls an empty
wine bottle
sending ripples
of ridicule.

"Bah! I'm no canibal
but a custodian
of Western Civilization."

At night
we go to bed
to make love,
but bloodthirsty thugs
smash windows
bash my brains
take my willing
mistress away.

O! Let them take her!
Take her away for good!

THE MARBLE EYE

The marble eye
is an ornament
coldly carved by a craftsman
to fill an empty socket
as a corpse fills a coffin.

It sheds no tear,
it warms to no love,
it glowers with no anger,
it burns with no hate.

Blind it is to all colours.

Around it there is no evil
to be whisked away
with the tail of a horse
like a pestering fly.

Oh! the marble eye —
if only my eyes
were made of marble!

RIDE UPON THE DEATH CHARIOT

They rode upon
the death chariot
to their Golgotha—
three vagrants
whose papers to be in Caesar's empire
were not in order.

The sun
shrivelled their bodies
in the mobile tomb
as airtight as canned fish.

We're hot!
We're thirsty!
We're hungry!

The centurion
touched their tongues
with the tip
of a lance
dipped in apathy:

"Don't cry to me
but to Ceasar who
crucifies you."

A woman came
to wipe their faces.
She carried a dishcloth
full of bread and tea.

We're dying!

The centurion
washed his hands.

[The allusion in this poem is to the death of three pass law "offenders" who suffocated in an overloaded police pick-up van which broke down on a hot day. The constables in charge refused to unlock the van and ignored the plight of their prisoners even though it was many hours before relief came. The pass law applies only to Africans and pass inspections, resulting in the arrest of any whose pass documents are "not in order", are a matter of routine: see *Always a Suspect.*—ed.]

DIRGE FOR MY PASSING YEARS

Standing on the sands of these years,
strolling on this desolate shore
where the night unfolds her eiderdown of darkness
                on my shivering body,

I look back at my past
staring over my shoulder like a one-eyed gargoyle.

My future is a tottering wall
lashed by the force of a human hurricane.

My hair jumps on end
as seagulls veer and swoop above my head
tearing my thoughts with jeering screams,
and billows brawl amongst themselves
as they race to pickle my voice in a bottle.

Their noise deafens me,
I shudder,
I quiver in terror,
I clutch my puny poetic fists
and punch wildly at the immense powers.

They laugh with hundredfold scorn.
I scream:
No sound comes out from a mouth
wide as the gates of hell.
I weep the reservoirs of tearducts dry
as a Vaal riverbed in a drought.

Where am I?
What am I?
Am I just a minute beetle hiding under a clod of sand
ready to be squashed by a white beachstroller's foot?

Vaal river forming the southern boundary of the Transvaal

My body writhes helplessly in a python's crush;
and my mind is strangled in the tentacles of an octopus.

I spit my last defiant hiss
and gasp the death breath
for freedom to be free.

Only a whirling brain remains alive drifting in a dark cloud
to a desert mirage of fleeting dreams
where a golden water jug pours into a cup
                                of unquenchable desires.

I grope nearer to snatch the water pitcher:
a policeman snaps his handcuffs on my wrists
and drags me into my hell
where I am left to chew spiders and scorpions
with a dry swollen tongue.

In the grave I meet my mother
black as ebony
smooth as ivory
sweett as syrup on a cake.
Her body lies embalmed
in a handkerchief of my tears.

My father is not there.
He had left me, a child,
with his penis to eat for a boerewors
and his testicles to slice as onion and tomato
to gravy my dry and stale mieliepap.

Boerewors   boer sausage (Afrikaans)

AMAGODUKA AT GLENCOE STATION

We travelled a long journey
through the wattle forests of Vryheid,
crossed the low-levelled Blood River
whose water flowed languidly
as if dispirited for the
shattered glory of my ancestors.

We passed the coalfields of Dundee —
blackheads in the wrinkled face
of Northern Zululand —
until our train ultimately came
to a hissing stop at Glencoe.

Many people got off
leaving the enraged train
to snort and charge at the night
on it's way to Durban.

The time was 8 p.m.

I picked up my suitcase,
sagging under the weight of a heavy overcoat
I shambled to the "non-European Males" waiting room.

The room was crowded
the air hung, a pall of choking odour,
rotten meat, tobacco and sour beer.

Windows were shut tight
against the sharp bite of winter.

Amagoduka   mine labor recruits (Zulu)

Amagoduka sat on bare floor
their faces sucking the warmth
of the coal fire crackling in the corner.

They chewed dried bread
scooped corned beef with rusty knives,
and drank *mgombothi* from the plastic can
which they passed from mouth to mouth.

They spoke animatedly
and laughed in thunderous peals.

A girl peeped through the door,
they shuddered at the sudden cold blast,
jumped up to fondle and leer at her
"*Hau! ngena Sisi!* — Oh! come in sister!"

She shied like a frightened filly
banged the door and bolted.
They broke into tumultuous laughter.

One of them picked up a guitar
plucked it with broken finger nails
caressed its strings with a castor oil bottle —

it sighed like a jilted girl.
"You play down! Phansi! Play D" he whispered.

Another joined in with a concertina,
it's sound fluttered in flowery notes
like a butterfly picking pollen from flower to flower.

The two began to sing,
their voices crying for the moutnains
and the hills of Msinga, stripped naked of
their green garment.

They crossed rivers and streams,
gouged dry by the sun rays,
where lowing cattle genuflected
for a blade of grass and a drop of water
on riverbeds littered with carcasses and bones.

They spoke of hollow-cheeked maidens
heaving drums of brackish water
from a far away fountain.

They told of big-bellied babies
sucking festering fingers
instead of their mothers shrivelled breasts.

Two cockroaches
as big as my overcoat buttons
jived across the floor
snatched meat and bread crumbs
and scurried back to their hideout.

The whole group joined in unison:
curious eyes peered through frosted windows
"Ekhaya bafowethu!—Home brothers!"

We come from across the Tugela river,
we are going to eGoli! eGoli! eGoli!
where they'll turn us into moles
that eat the gold dust
and spit out blood.

eGoli   Zulu name for Johannesburg

SOUNDS OF A COWHIDE DRUM

Boom! Boom! Boom!
I hear it far in the northern skies —
a rumble and a roar as of thunder.

I prick my ears
like a buck ready to flee from an imminent storm.

Boom! Boom! Boom!
As it rolls nearer
and nearer to the southern sky
it holds my heart,
my hopes soaring high into the eagle's throne.

Boom! Boom! Boom!
I am the drum on your dormant soul,
cut from the black hide of a sacrificial cow.

I am the spirit of your ancestors,
habitant in hallowed huts,
eager to protect,
forever vigilant.

Let me tell you of your precious heritage,
of your glorious past trampled by the conqueror,
destroyed by the zeal of a missionary.

I lay bare facts for scrutiny
by your searching mind,
all declarations and dogmas.

O! Hear me, Child!
in the Zulu dance
shaking their hearts into a frenzy.

O! Hear me, Child!
in the night vigils of black Zionists
lifting their spirits into ecstasy.

Boom! Boom! Bom!
That is the sound of a cowhide drum—
the Voice of Mother Africa.

We'll live in compounds
where young men are pampered
into partners for older men.

We'll visit shebeens
where a whore waits for a fee
to leave your balls burning
with syphilitic fire.

If the gods are with us—
Oh! beloved black gods of our forefathers
What have we done to you
Why have you forsaken us—
We'll return home
to find our wives nursing babies—
unknown to us
but only to their mothers and loafers.

shebeen unlicensed drinking house, particularly important during the
period when South African law prohibited hard liquor for Africans.
(from Irish)